AMERICAN *Sculptors* SERIES

———————— 2 ————————

PAUL
MANSHIP

———— NEW YORK ————

W · W · NORTON & COMPANY · INC ·
UNDER THE AUSPICES OF
THE NATIONAL SCULPTURE SOCIETY

Cover photograph: Playfulness, small bronze, 1912

PAUL
MANSHIP

Paul Manship

Credo

The credo of the artist is the result of his education and environment. He cannot depart from his age and its spiritual and material influences. His handwriting is established in the formative years of youth, but though it may improve in clarity and forcefulness with time, its basic character remains the exposition of his temperament and intelligence.

Early studies of Classical and Renaissance sculpture helped to form the technical approach to the problems of my art. And my taste and understanding were influenced by the masterful achievements of the artists of antiquity.

Sculpture is but a part of the greater scheme of art—dissociated from Nature, it still must find its rhythms in the organization of natural forms. Architecture and its abstract forms also belong to this large scheme to which the sculptor should devote his studies. But more important than formalities and geometrical considerations is the feeling for human qualities and harmony and movement of life.

The magnitude of artistic inspiration in the forms and moods of Nature is infinite. The possibility of realizing it in sculpture has endless approaches. Materials and techniques await but hands to use them and skills to turn ideas and emotions into objects of beauty or expression.

The stimulation of desire to create gives wings to the artist's inspiration. The inadequacies and limitations of power of visualization and training in technique keep his feet to earth.

Of such things is made the Great Excitement and Mystery of Art.

PAUL MANSHIP

Little Brother, small bronze, 1913

Baby Pauline Manship, marble, Metropolitan Museum of Art, New York, 1912

Dancer and Gazelles, bronze, approximately 30″ high, 1916

9

John D. Rockefeller, portrait bust, marble, 1918

Armillary Sphere, bronze, 26″ diameter, 1920

ERECTED·BY·THE·MUSEUM
IN·GRATEFUL·REMEMBRANCE
·OF·THE·SERVICES·OF·
JOHN
PIERPONT
MORGAN
FROM·1871·TO·1913
AS·TRUSTEE·BENEFACTOR
·AND·PRESIDENT·
HE·WAS·IN·ALL·RESPECTS
A·GREAT·CITIZEN··HE
HELPED·TO·MAKE·NEW·YORK
THE·TRUE·METROPOLIS
OF·AMERICA·HIS·INTEREST
IN·ART·WAS·LIFELONG·
HIS·GENEROUS·DEVOTION
TO·IT·COMMANDED·WORLD·
WIDE·APPRECIATION·
HIS·MUNIFICENT·GIFTS·TO
THE·MUSEUM·ARE·AMONG
ITS·CHOICEST·TREASURES
VITA·PLENA
LABORIS
M·C·M·X·X

Memorial to John Pierpont Morgan, stone, 12′ high, Metropolitan Museum of Art, 1920

12

LITERATURE

Detail from the Morgan Memorial opposite

Europa, stone, 2′ long, 1924

Flight of Europa, bronze, gold leaf patina, approximately 30″ long, 1925

Actaeon, bronze, heroic size, companion to Diana opposite, Brookgreen Gardens, Georgetown, S. C., 1924

16

Diana, bronze, heroic size, 1924

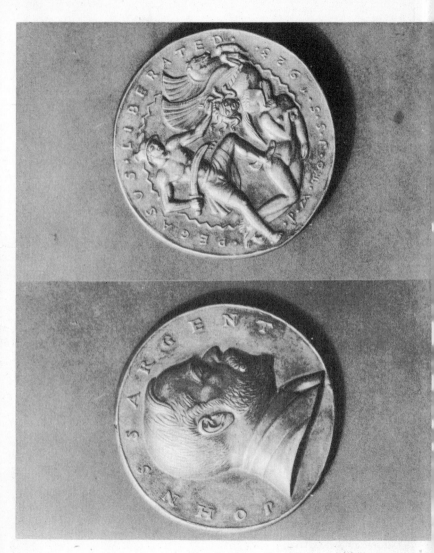

Bronze medal, portrait of John Singer Sargent on obverse, *Pegasus Liberated* on reverse, 1923

Lady Chalmondeley, portrait bust, 1923

19

Monument in the American Cemetery at Thiancourt, France, stone, 1926

Fame, pink Georgia marble, 27″, detail from monument opposite, 1926

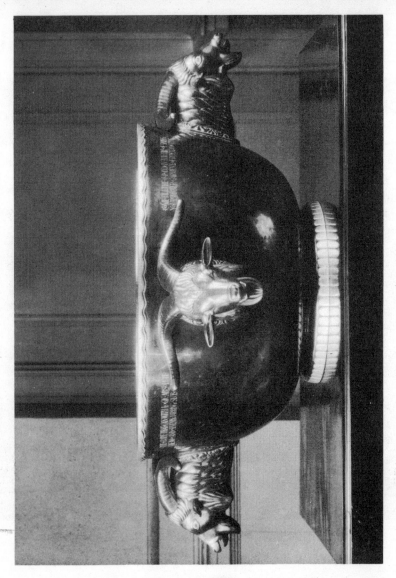

Punch Bowl, The Century Club, New York, 1928

Baboon, bronze, detail from the Paul Rainey Memorial Gate, New York Zoological Park, 1933

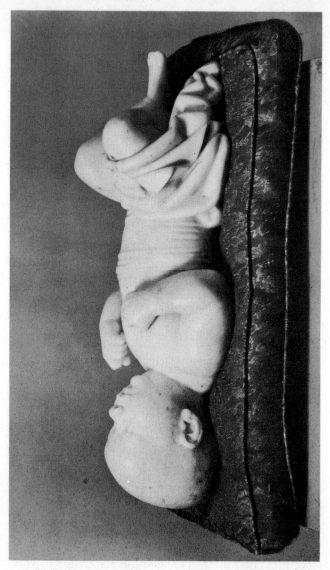

Sarah Jane Manship, age 3 months, marble, 1930

24

Baby Vivian Stanley Clark, marble, 1934

Leopard, bronze with silver and gold inlay, 1933

Owl, bronze, detail from the Paul Rainey Memorial gate, New York Zoological Park, 1933

Deer, bronze, heroic size, 1933

Three Bears, bronze, 34" high, 1935

Detail from Paul J. Rainey Memorial bronze entrance gate, 35' high, New York Zoological Park, 1933

Detail from Paul J. Rainey Memorial bronze entrance gate, 35' high, New York
Zoological Park, 1933

Bronze entrance gate to the New York Zoological Park, Paul J. Rainey Memorial, 1933

Time and the Fates, sundial, 48' high, New York World's Fair, 1939-1940

33

Lincoln the Hoosier Youth, bronze, heroic size, Fort Wayne, Indiana, 1934

Justice, bronze, detail from base of statue, "Lincoln the Hoosier Youth," Fort Wayne, Indiana, 1933

John Manship, marble, 1933

Venus Anadyomene, marble, Phillips Academy, Andover, Mass., 1935

Prometheus, bronze, heroic size, Rockefeller Center, New York, 1934

Pegasus, bronze, 1936

Sketch for equestrian statue of General James Longstreet for the battlefield at Gettysburg, Pa., 1938

The Parting of General Lee and Stonewall Jackson on the Eve of Chancellorsville,
sketch for equestrian statue, 1936

Celestial Sphere, bronze, 13′6″ in diameter, Woodrow Wilson Memorial, League of Nations, Geneva, Switzerland, 1939

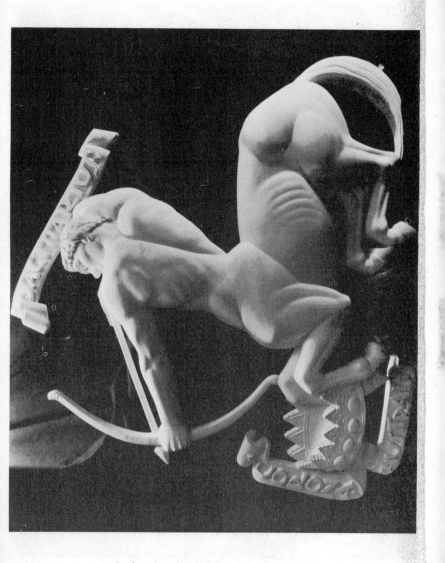

Sagittarius, detail from Celestial Sphere

Leo, detail from Celestial Sphere

Orion, detail from Celestial Sphere

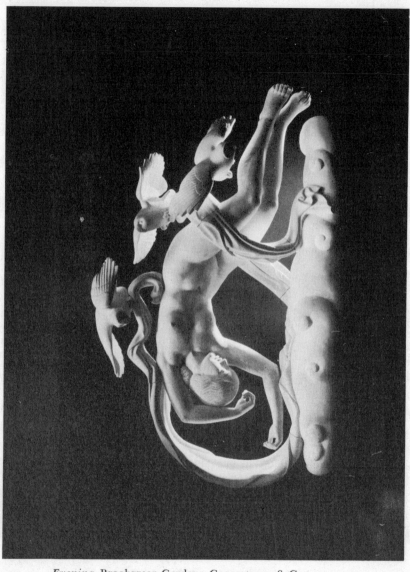

Evening, Brookgreen Gardens, Georgetown, S. C., 1939-1940

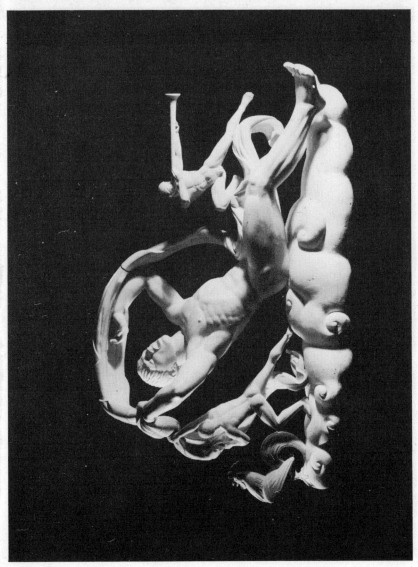

Morning, for World's Fair, New York, 1939-1940

Night, for World's Fair, New York, 1939-1940

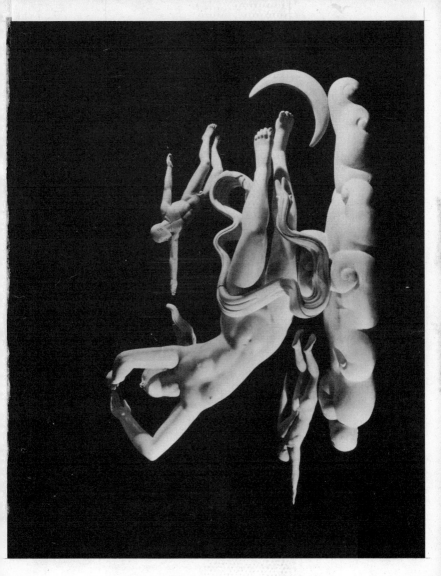

Night, for World's Fair, New York, 1938

In Loving Memory of

OTIS
SKINNER

1858   1942

Good Night
Sweet Prince
and Flights of Angels
Sing Thee to thy Rest

Otis Skinner Memorial, terra cotta, 1943

Garden of Eden, sundial, bronze, 1943

Sarah Jane Manship, marble, 1945

Sarah Jane, bas relief, 1944

Van Wyck Brooks, terra cotta, 1945

Gifford Beal, 1945

Preston Pope Satterwhite, M.D., marble, 1946

Sir Douglas Alexander, marble, 1946

Albert A. Murphree, bronze, heroic size, on the campus of the University of Florida, Gainesville, Florida, 1946

Eagle Lectern, wood, 1947

Biographical Sketch

Born at St. Paul, Minnesota, on December 25, 1885, to Charles
Henry and Maryetta (Friend) Manship

Art Education: St. Paul Institute of Art; Pennsylvania Academy
of Fine Arts; American Academy in Rome

Married: Isabel McIlwaine of New York City

Children: Pauline F. H., Elizabeth R., John P., Sarah Jane

Membership:

    National Academy of Design
    Fellow, National Sculpture Society (President 1939-1942)
    American Academy of Arts and Letters
    Alumni Association, American Academy in Rome (President)
    National Fine Arts Commission
    Fellow, American Academy of Arts and Sciences
    Corresponding member, National Academy of Fine Arts,
        Argentina, 1944
    Corresponding member, Academy of Beaux Arts,
        Institute of France, 1946

Clubs:

    Century
    National Arts (New York)
    L'Union Interalliée (Paris)
    Arts (Washington)

Awards

Helen Barnett Prize of the National Academy of Design, 1913 and 1917; George D. Widener Memorial Gold Medal of the Pennsylvania Academy, 1914; Gold Medal, San Francisco Exposition, 1915; Gold Medal, American Institute of Architects, 1921; American Numismatic Society Medal, 1924; Gold Medal of the Philadelphia Art Week, 1925; Gold Medal, Sesquicentennial Exposition, Philadelphia, 1926; Diplôme d'honneur, Paris Exposition, 1937; Medal of Honor, National Sculpture Society, 1942; Gold Medal for Sculpture, National Institute of Arts and Letters, 1944

Decorated: Legion of Honor (France), 1929

Works

Represented in the Metropolitan Museum of Art, New York City; Pratt Institute, Brooklyn, N. Y.; Detroit Museum of Arts; Minneapolis Art Museum; Art Institute of Chicago; St. Louis Art Museum; Musé de Luxembourg, Paris, France, etc.

Notable Works:

Morgan Memorial, The Metropolitan Museum, New York City

Sculpture at Phillips Academy, Andover, Mass.

Rainey Memorial Gateway, New York Zoological Park, New York City, 1933

Bronze statue of Lincoln as a young man, Ft. Wayne, Indiana, 1932

Woodrow Wilson Memorial, League of Nations, Geneva, Switzerland, 1939